To abandon oneself
    in the dance with a horse
is to touch the Infinite.

conversations with
horse

*an uncommon dialog of
equine wisdom*

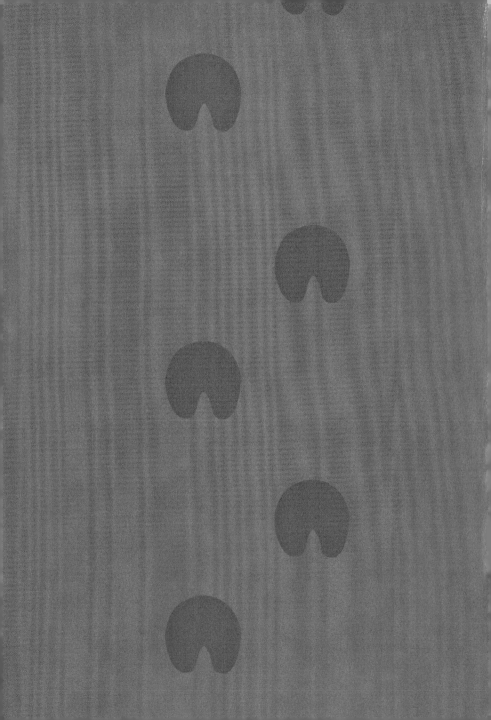

conversations with

horse

an uncommon dialog of equine wisdom

Kate Solisti-Mattelon

Council Oak Books
San Francisco / Tulsa

Council Oak Books, LLC
San Francisco / Tulsa
www.counciloakbooks.com

Cover and interior photos © 2004 Tony Stromberg
Cover and interior design by Buffy Terry
Typesetting by Vanessa Perez

Printed in Canada

First printing 2004

Library of Congress Cataloging-in-Publication Data

Solisti-Mattelon, Kate.
  Conversations with horse : an uncommon dialog of equine wisdom / Kate Solisti-Mattelon.
      p. cm.
  Originally published: Hillsboro, Or. : Beyond Words Pub., c2003.
  ISBN 1-57178-157-9
  1. Horses—Behavior—Miscellanea. 2. Human-animal communication—Miscellanea. I. Title.
  SF281.S65 2004
  636.1—dc22
                                        2004016899
ISBN 1-57158-157-9

Also by

Kate Solisti-Mattelon

Conversations with Cat

Conversations with Dog

The Holistic Animal Handbook

Kinship with the Animals

Contents

Acknowledgments

I'm deeply grateful to the Council of Equines for sharing their wisdom through me. It's an honor and a privilege to be their "voice" in these pages.

I wish to thank Shelley Donnelly, who introduced me to the "energetic horse" and helped me ask the questions that led her to develop a remarkable body of healing work with and for the horse.

Thanks go to all the people who sent in questions for this book: Charly Lally, Ben Day, Jens Uwe F. Buschmann, Bob and Debbi Sencenbaugh, Ellen Kemper, Pamela Stones, Kelly Nichols, Cheryl Fox, Kathy Newman, Robin Stark, Betsy Cullen, Joni Gang, Anna and Karl Fisher, Shelley Donnelly, Helen Wells, Gail Corle, Devta Khalsa, Marija Krunic, Oteka Brab, Zoe D'ay, and Miranda Solisti.

Special thanks to Heidi Grimditch and her horses, especially Secret.

Thanks to all at Council Oak Books for loving this book. Thanks Tony Stromberg for your magnificent photographs and to Buffy Terry and Vanessa Perez for designing this beautiful book. And thanks to Linda Tellington-Jones for her glowing remarks and for her support of me and my work since 1993.

Special gratitude goes to my cousin, Carey Churchill Cort, one of my best childhood friends and the person who made it possible for me to know Coke, the horse who taught me that trusting a horse can lead one to connect with All-That-Is, to feel what it's like to fully surrender and to be carried out of time by Pegasus.

And thank you, Patrice, my husband and partner. Our love and our marriage make all things possible!

To

Katan and his parents,
Twilight and Klassique

Twilight worked hard to become the perfect mother, and Klassique, a Master Teacher in horse form, is fathering special horses who are generating healing all over the world. Katan, their son, the perfect light of his parents' spirits, is a teacher and an inspiration. I am truly honored to know you and to be able to share your journeys and wisdom with humans who care.

And thank you Andrea for asking me to be your horses' "voices."

introduction

Horses have had a unique relationship with humanity through the ages. In most cultures horses abound across ancient myths. Symbolically, horses have simultaneously represented our higher mind and our deepest passions. Once hunted for food, horses next became domesticated as helpers and "beasts of burden." Humans learned to respect horses for their strength. Later we learned to cherish them for their special gifts and we highly valued them as partners and companions in work, in war, and in life. More recently, we seemed to lull ourselves into treating them as expensive, beautiful objects to be used, bought, and sold. What is the next step in our relationship with horse?

I believe that we are on the brink of renewing our partnership with horses. Many guardians, teachers, and more and more trainers are seeking to shift from objectifying the horse to rekindling a true relationship with the horse. We are at a critical moment in our evolution as spiritual beings. Are we ready to embrace the equine's spiritual essence?

Horse. The very word brings to mind power, beauty, wildness, freedom, and passion. Who are these beings? They are flesh, blood, bone, and spirit. Horses are individuated souls, growing and evolving from one life to the next, just as humans are. Horses are capable of complex thoughts, emotions, and decisions. They are fiercely loyal and committed. They give us tremendous gifts, if we only allow ourselves to be open to them.

Like us, horses experience the physical realities of pleasure, pain, hormonal impulses, birth, life, and death. They experience emotions such as joy and grief. Unlike us, however, horses live every day in a state of oneness with all beings on the planet. Do horses know they do this? Of course! In fact, the mission of the horse—in sacred service to the planet—is to help us remember that we are living in a state of oneness too. How can horses teach us? They teach us in many ways, all leading back to love. When a horse is in partnership with a human being, both beings grow physically, mentally, emotionally, and spiritually. Horses express love through trust. Only when a horse fully trusts a human, and this human fully trusts a horse, can we experience the oneness with creation that a horse feels.

Today, perhaps more than ever before, people are longing for connection. People are adopting animals by the hundreds, longing to find companionship and love in the midst of their busy, challenging lives. Being an animal guardian means that we are fully responsible for the life of another. Like an infant, our animals are almost completely dependent on us for their food, shelter, and well-being. Humans are usually good at caring for others. We are encoded to care. It can be argued that we need to care for others. If we don't learn how to do this, we are rarely happy. Caring for others stimulates our compassion and enables us to inhabit a world rich in diverse personalities. We are stimulated to feel, think, and take action. When we feel connected to others, we know that we are alive. When we are alive, we can ask the question, "Who are we and who are these beings who love us so much?"

Our ancestors recognized that interdependency creates balance and life. When the human race was younger, we learned and received many gifts from species other than our own. We respected animals as healers and teachers. But as time passed, people began losing this connection with other species and with Mother Earth. As a result, today much of humanity feels discontented, purposeless, unhappy, unfulfilled, fragmented, and alone. But at last, many are searching for meaning and connection. We're coming back around.

Stories exist in every human culture about the deep connection we once enjoyed with the natural world. Some stories tell of how we became separate and isolated from other species and from Mother Earth. I received such a story about three species who chose to remain with us to help us remember who we truly are. It goes like this:

Once, in the beginning of time, there existed a council of beings who represented different expressions of the Creator in all sorts of marvelous forms. Around the council fire sat representatives from the insect, reptile, bird, mammal, marsupial, and human families. Each shared his story about how his species incarnated to experience life in a particular form, in order to learn and to share specific truths with all other beings. The common goal was to better understand—together—ourselves and our Creator. Turtle chose its form to learn how to cooperate with water and land. Lion chose to experience family teamwork and the partnership between predator and prey. Dolphin connected earth and sky with water and kept its mind open to the cosmos. Humans chose to explore our remarkable intellect, manual dexterity, and ability for spoken language.

In the beginning, every being was connected heart to heart as one family. They enjoyed sharing their new experiences of life in their chosen forms. But one day, we humans stopped returning to the council fire. Consumed by our own accomplishments, we forgot that we had agreed to share our experiences with the other beings. As we became more separate, we began to feel superior; we began to forget that we were all one family. A chasm was created between ourselves and the other creatures. Most of the other animals continued on their own paths, but three species lingered, determined to mend the ever-widening gap between humans and other creatures. At a critical moment, the horse, the cat, and the dog consciously chose to leave the comfort of their fellow creatures, to a great extent, and accompany the humans, hoping to lead us back to the Creator, back to connection, back to Love. To this day, we have only to stop and pay attention and these three will remind us of who we truly are.

In this special moment in time, we can stop and ask horses what they think of their relationships with humans and what they are up to with us. What an opportunity!

Communication with horses, as described in this book, goes beyond the parameters of equine brain size, physical capabilities, instincts, and behavior. I am not concerned with proving that equine consciousness as I've experienced it is measurable by human standards and technologies. This book is about tapping into the Divine Consciousness that operates in and through every living being, stone, and body of water on our planet.

Each unique species and individual expresses Divine Consciousness in his or her own way. I have not interviewed individual horses for this book. Rather, I've connected with the Council of Equines, or higher group consciousness of all horses, in order to get the "big picture" as opposed to individual opinions. In this book, I approach horses from our shared spiritual connection. In this place of unity, there is no need for spoken language. Divine Consciousness is expressed as a language of the heart, as interspecies communication and understanding. The information in *Conversations with Horse* is not definitive for all horses, for all time. I am a vehicle for this information with my own filter system. I'm only as clear a receiver as my consciousness level at this time allows. As with most information we humans share with one another, the final proof of its usefulness comes through testing it against our own life experiences. I encourage you to filter this information through your own relationship with your horse to determine its "truth."

Conversations with Horse introduces the reader to the spiritual, physical, emotional, and mental awareness inherent in the equine species. Individual levels of awareness vary from horse to horse, just as they do from person to person. This book is not a horse-care manual. It is a tool for deeper understanding.

It is my hope that books such as *Conversations with Horse, Conversations with Cat,* and *Conversations with Dog* can help people remember how to tap into the Divine Consciousness in horses, cats, dogs, ferrets, sparrows, turtles, lions—all of Creation: animal, vegetable, and mineral—and so share our experiences once again as ancient legends say was intended. I will continue to use my gift to support and encourage all kinds of interspecies communication in order to deepen understanding and connection between all beings. For me, it's all about Love.

When I wrote *Conversations with Dog,* I was deeply touched by canine wisdom expressed with constant gentle compassion for us human beings. As I sat down to talk with cats for *Conversations with Cat,* an entirely different energy emerged. Cats tell it like it is! In *Conversations with Horse,* horses ask us to be equal partners, and they shed light on how we all benefit from understanding each other better. Read together, these three books give voice to these extraordinary beings who are committed to helping humanity find our way back Home. How truly blessed we are to live in the company of animals. Enjoy!

earthly beings with *universal* understanding

chapter one

"Horses lend us the wings we lack."

—Pam Brown

Horses, as a species, have committed to bringing us back to unity with ourselves and with other physical beings on our planet. They give us many gifts, but perhaps the greatest gift of all is to teach us trust.

Trust can only occur between two willing beings. For a human to understand trust, she needs to surrender herself to another. When a human surrenders herself to a horse and that horse, in turn, surrenders himself to her, something extraordinary takes place. Hearts and minds open. The human has only to think of what she wants her horse to do and he does it. Communication takes place seamlessly, effortlessly. Horse and rider become one. As this happens, the horse will carry his rider into a place of unity with all life, what has been called the "Cosmic Dance." If you are privileged enough to enjoy this experience with your horse, you have a glimpse into the ecstatic reunion with Life, Love, and the Creator. This is the great gift from horse.

How many riders experience this unity? During the last one hundred years or so, riders were trained to control and dominate their horses. This theory is based on a basic fear that the horse will harm the rider or misbehave and embarrass the rider in competition. Trainers taught riders that the horse was little more than a mindless vehicle. The rider needed to be the brains, the driver. In this mind-set, the horse is asked to respond only to physical signals from his rider. He isn't asked to think because these trainers believe that horses are not capable of thoughts or decisions beyond basic survival instincts. Horse and rider training consisted of endless repeated exercises to drill movements into the mind of the rider and into the body of the horse. What is the result of such a technique? A horse severely limited by human fear and control and a rider severely limited by his own mental and physical abilities.

Fortunately, in the last decade or so there has been an outburst of natural training techniques designed to return to ways of respecting horses and riding in partnership with them. One definition of partnership is "two persons dancing together." When two people dance together, there is communication, a respect for one another's strengths and weaknesses, and an intense focus on listening to one another's bodies so

Be willing to allow horse to fly.

that the two move as one. This partnership is based on trust. Our opportunity as "horse people" is to find that dance between us and our horses. It's an intimate, personal experience, ultimately one that has the potential to deeply enrich both of us—but only if we're willing to allow our horse to "fly" and to ask her to teach us how we can fly together.

This is how it happened for me. When I was fourteen, I spent some weeks with my cousin Carey and her family on their farm in northern New Jersey. Carey's parents had bought her a majestic dark bay thoroughbred named Bracken. How gorgeous he was! I was in awe of him and a bit jealous of all Carey and Bracken could do together. Fortunately for me, Carey's parents had also bought a chestnut quarterhorse named Coke. It was a magical time for me! In addition to taking care of chickens and beautiful red rabbits, I learned how to ride.

The first time I got on Coke's back I was really scared. I felt so high and vulnerable. Coke demonstrated his experience and stood perfectly still and calm. Carey showed me how to hold the reins, explaining that Coke had been a ranch horse and had a very strong mouth. I didn't have to be afraid to pull back pretty hard to tell him I wanted him to stop. She told me that Coke would listen to my body more than to my voice, so I needed to communicate what I wanted him to do by moving my body forward and squeezing with my legs when I wanted him to move and by sitting heavy and back slightly when I wanted him to slow down or to stop.

Carey said, "OK, walk." I said, "How do I get him to walk?" She said, "It's easy. Squeeze with your knees." It worked, and we walked. Carey said, "Great, now trot." I said, "Trot?" She said, "Give him a little kick." Afraid to hurt him, I squeezed and kicked a little. Coke broke into a trot. I grinned. Carey said, "Post, like this..." and she demonstrated a graceful rising with the horse. Wow! I got it instantly. Coke and I were moving together. Before I had a chance to really savor this moment, Carey ordered, "Canter, like this!" I kicked again, and we broke into a glorious canter with Carey and the beautiful Bracken right beside us. "OK, gallop!" she yelled, and we were off!

I didn't have time to be afraid. I felt Coke connecting to me and I to him. The next thing I knew, Carey was reining me in, and we slowed and stopped. I was speechless and really proud of myself! I could ride!

My aunt came running out of the house scolding Carey for what she had done. Perhaps Carey had rushed things a bit, but it was the best way for her to teach me. If she'd gone any slower, my fears and considerable self-doubts would have gotten the better of me and I might never have learned to ride. Carey's fast-speed lesson enabled me to feel capable and unafraid. My body seemed to have a natural affinity for the horse's body. And, perhaps most important of all, Coke was happy to be my steady, dependable teacher.

> *My body had a natural affinity for the horse's body.*

The next weeks were magical. Carey and I rode every day. We played hide-and-seek on horseback in the two-hundred-year-old fields bordered by ancient stone fences. We played cowgirls and pretended to round up the cows.

We raced each other home up the cow pasture. She always had to give me a head start since Coke was no match for Bracken, the thoroughbred. Carey and Bracken always won, but the thrill of racing up the hill and into the yard was wonderful. One time, as Carey and Bracken passed me at full speed, he kicked up a cow patty, which hit me squarely in the chest and then dropped down between me and the saddle. I let out a whoop and Carey looked back. We both laughed so hard, we practically fell off as we made it to the barn. Again my aunt rushed out. She took one look at me and burst into laughter as well. I was covered with cow manure from neck to knees. What a mess! What a glorious time!

Coke and I were really bonding. As Carey brushed and groomed the beautiful Bracken, I brushed and groomed the old quarterhorse. He loved the attention. One day we rode in a new direction to go swimming at a neighbor's house. My aunt drove the car slowly down the country road, and we followed. We arrived, tied up the horses, and went for a swim. Afterward, my aunt asked if we remembered the way home. Carey said she did, but I had no idea. My aunt left, and Carey and I got on the horses.

Carey decided to "go the back way," hoping she'd remember how to get home. Somehow, on the way home, we got separated. I stopped and called her. No answer. My normal response would have been to panic, but this time I didn't. I put my arms around Coke's neck and said, "OK, boy, I trust you to take us home." Coke's energy shifted under me. His body felt different. I instinctively melted into him. He began to walk and then trot. I posted like a pro. Then he began to canter. At that point something happened. Time and place disappeared. All that existed was Coke and me. We were totally one. My heart and his heart beat together. His body and mine merged. We seemed to be flying through space. I didn't feel the ground beneath us—just our muscles and strong breathing as he raced home with me. All of a sudden we were standing calmly at the barn gate. I didn't want to get off. I don't know how long we stood there reentering the world as I had previously known it. When Carey

Time and space disappeared. We were totally one.

appeared, I reluctantly got down and took off Coke's saddle. Nobody spoke. I led Coke into the barn and looked into his eyes. He gave me the most loving, deep look that touched my soul, and then he bent down and ate his supper.

The feeling I experienced that day was so profound, I have never forgotten it. I never spoke about it to anyone for many years because it was intensely personal, for one thing. I also had no words to describe what I felt. I wasn't sure anybody would understand, and it was too great a treasure to share with nonbelievers! I just knew that in that special moment, Coke and I had merged into one being. I was no longer a girl riding a horse on a country road on a summer afternoon. There was no country road, no girl, no horse, just one energy—one energy that was part of everything. It was pure joy. Pure freedom. Pure love.

Many years later I remembered my ability to connect with animals at this deep level. I began "hearing" animals' thoughts and feelings and receiving mental pictures from them. This was a memory from my first six years when I was open and listening to plants and animals all the time. But I had literally shut off this ability when I was between six and eight after the death of my beloved cat, Dusty. (The details of my story with Dusty appear in *Conversations with Cat*.) While growing up, I tried to banish the memories, but I was still haunted by the deep discussions Dusty and I had shared. Of course, I rarely spoke about this to anyone. Then, in my late twenties, I began to "hear" by way of sensing the thoughts and feelings of non-human beings again. This time I refused to close my mind. The feeling of connection was so heart-opening, I knew that I had to pursue these communications. I developed and refined my intuitive "muscle," which was the seat of this receiving. As I did so, I was once again swept into a oneness. It was a softer feeling than the dramatic, passionate feeling I'd experienced with Coke. Nevertheless, it was profound, and I knew that my life's work was to share these communications from the animal and plant kingdoms with whoever was ready to listen.

A few years into developing my abilities as an animal communicator, I met a woman named Shelley Donnelly, who was living in France. Shelley contacted me to invite me to help her develop an energetic healing modality for animals. She wanted an animal communicator to explore her concepts with the animals she was hoping to help.

With trust there can be surrender, release, and a merging into love and oneness.

Shelley "tested" me to be sure I was the right person for the job. Her Italian Greyhound, Fiorino, was the one who ultimately had the final say as to whether I was the one for the job. Fortunately for me, Fiorino approved. I picked up the work on dogs and horses where an extremely gifted French psychic, Cathy Girod, had left off. Shelley and I spent four years working together learning about animals from their point of view.

We worked with what I refer to as the Council of Equines, the Council of Canines, and the Council of Felines. These councils represent the higher mind and group soul of the particular animals. This way, we were able to get the highest, most pure information since it didn't have to pass through any individual horses, dogs, or cats. The questions in this book were posed to this same Council. Shelley and I learned a great deal about who horses truly are and what their relationship with humans is about. I became the student of these gifted teachers. In the course of exploring the horse, I learned about what happened between Coke and me when I was fourteen.

The Council of Equines taught us that horses have a relationship with humans to teach us about trust. Trust is the foundation of Love. With trust, there can be surrender, release, and a merging into love and oneness. A lack of trust keeps us separate and afraid. Oh, the irony of that information! As I looked around at the competitive horse "world," I saw legions of trainers, instructors, and riding schools focusing on teaching humans to dominate horses, to be the brains, while the horse should be the brawn, the vehicle, for getting the rider where he needed to go. Where was trust being learned or encouraged? How could trust grow when the ego of the rider and/or trainer superceded even the well-being of the horse? In this environment, horses suffer innumerable physical and emotional pains. How could the horse accomplish his mission when we humans were blinded to the opportunity for connection through trust? After all these years of non-recognition, why were horses still incarnating to be with humans?

I learned from the Council of Equines that horses carry the quality of idealism. One definition of idealism is "persistent hopefulness." Horses are persistently hopeful that humanity will wake up and remember how to honor the gifts horses bring and learn how to reconnect to the oneness that is our birthright. When I surrendered myself

to Coke in complete trust, he gave his heart to me and
together we experienced this merging, an ecstatic union
with life.

HORSE'S TEACHING BEGINS WITH OUR PAYING ATTENTION

How do we learn to tune in to this trust, this love?
The first step is to wake up and be present with our horses. The next step is to help them wake up and realize that
we wish to go to this level
with them. Many horses
have had to shut down
their open hearts because
we've not allowed them to
be themselves. We have not

Horses are persistently hopeful that humanity will wake up.

entered into our relationship with them out of friendship
and respect. Through training methods, we've learned how
to control horses and bend them to our will. Perhaps some
of us have gone a bit farther and asked them to cooperate
with us and follow our commands. If we've really invested
time and patience getting to know our horses, then we
begin to see what remarkable individuals they are. We
begin to respect their individual personalities, desires, and
needs. We begin to pay attention to their bodies and
rhythms. We start to know them. Hopefully, we start to
love them. How many of you really love your horses?

11

Without love, you'll never have the experience I had with Coke. With love, all things are possible!

This is not a new concept. The Comanche, Nez Perce, and other Native American peoples had extraordinary partnerships with their horses. Like Mongolian tribesmen, cavalry officers, and knights, they depended on their horses to keep them safe in battle and when hunting large game like buffalo. In Europe, you can find statues erected to individual warhorses by officers and generals who loved and respected a special horse for his bravery and decisiveness in battle. Many times, these warhorses gave their lives to save their riders. Here is historical evidence of love and trust. It has not been lost—just forgotten.

where do we look for answers to our *questions?*

chapter two

"And God took a handful of southerly wind and blew His breath over it and created the horse."

—Bedouin saying

We human beings have been graced with teachers and sages who have helped us understand ourselves and find meaning in our lives. These wise teachers were "experts" in the human experience. But how many of them understood the experiences and perspectives of other species?

Today, communication between humans is becoming easier and easier. Language is not the barrier it once was, because computer technology is capable of almost instantaneous translation. However, we still are members of different cultures with different experiences of reality. To truly understand each other, we must make some effort to understand and appreciate our differences. Although this seems a commonsense approach to human relationships, we continue to expect animals to adjust and bend to our human culture with little adjustment or acceptance of their ways on our part. This has been defined as anthropocentric, which means "interpreting reality in terms of human values and experiences." What if we stepped out of our anthropocentrism and made the effort to learn more about the experiences of animals or if we went even deeper to learn their language? Wouldn't this broaden our perspectives and understanding of the world in dramatic new ways? What could we learn if we opened our hearts and minds to other non-human realities? Perhaps by understanding how animals perceive us and the world we share, we'll learn more about ourselves and our relationship to all animals and to our planet.

If you love animals and/or live with them, you experience interspecies communication all the time. You know how to "read" your horse's body language directed at you. You understand your horse's different vocalizations. Often she has a special call she uses just for you. Start paying more attention to the unique signals your horse sends you, and you will begin to realize how well you really understand her, and she you.

Do you have a special voice you use with your horse? What do you see in your horse that is different from other horses you've known? Now that you're thinking about how well you and your horse really do understand each other, let's go to the next level. Observe and

Start paying attention to the signals your horse sends.

approach your horse with this new awareness that you two are communicating all the time.

Horses are extremely sensitive beings on many levels. Because they're so large, we often assume that they don't feel pleasurable touch or pain as we do. This is completely incorrect. A horse has a very highly tuned body and energy field. It's important to remember that horses are prey animals. Because they are prey animals, they need to be acutely aware of what's going on around them. This heightened awareness has allowed them to survive as a species. In their relationships with humans, it can be both a blessing and a challenge. As prey animals, they need to be on the alert for fluctuations in their environment. They need to be able to rapidly determine if these fluctuations are threats or not. To perceive these subtle changes in their environment, they use their sense of smell as well as their energy field, which acts as an antenna or early warning system to alert them when danger comes near. Similar to a big bubble surrounding them, this energy field can be held very close to their physical bodies in order to pass undetected by others, or it can be expanded quite far. Individual horses in a herd will link up their energy fields, creating a larger bubble of energy around the entire herd. This supports weak horses as well as strengthens the entire herd's ability to sense approaching danger. This is one of the unseen ways all herd and flock animals help protect each other.

All living beings have an energy field, or aura. When your horse looks at you, he not only sees your physical body, but he also perceives and reads your energy field, which surrounds your physical body. In fact, what he reads in your energy field is usually what he responds to first. Your energy field contains a blueprint of your emotional, mental, and physical balance and well-being. Horses read our moods and our very thoughts as they tune in to our energy field. They have to. Their survival in the wild depended on reading the air for predators as well as sizing up other horses as friends or competitors. Although you may not perceive yourself or other humans as potential predators, the horse's cellular memory is designed to help him to discern whether or not anyone who approaches him is friend or foe. Remember that at one time, before we "domesticated" horses, we hunted them. Horses are still sensitive to the unspoken intentions of all who approach them. As such, they are usually excellent judges of human character!

Here's an illustration of a horse "reading" the energy field of a human being. You may have had an experience with your horse that goes something like this: You hear about a fabulous trainer. You invite him to come look at your horse to see if he'll take you both on. Your horse is out in the paddock, peacefully munching after spending a quiet time with you getting groomed and ready to meet the new trainer. As the trainer approaches your horse, she picks up her head, snorts, and goes on "red alert." You notice her agitation and get irritated because you hoped she'd be on her best behavior in order to impress the trainer. The closer he gets to your horse, the more agitated she becomes. What is your horse reacting to? She is picking up something in the trainer's body language, energy field, or thoughts that threaten her or make her uncomfortable. By her agitation, she's telling you that this trainer is threatening her and possibly you too. Do you pay attention to your horse's signals?

Horses are sensitive to unspoken intentions.

Scenario 1. You decide that she's responding this way because you're both nervous. Even though after the trainer leaves you have this gnawing feeling that something isn't "right," you choose to disregard your gut feelings and your horse's messages. You sign up with the trainer. As lessons begin, you and your horse struggle to learn. You feel your trust and partnership with your horse being undermined. The trainer pushes his agenda. You follow even though you're stressed and frustrated. Your horse is miserable. Injury to her or to you follows. You stop training, feel incompetent, give up riding, and sell your horse.

Scenario 2. You think about your horse's response to the trainer. You go to her, stroke her, and talk to her. She calms down. Your intuition tells you that this trainer isn't right for you or your horse. You pay attention and trust your gut feeling and your horse's messages. You tell her that he won't be working with you both and thank her for letting you know that she felt uncomfortable with the trainer. You promise to find a trainer about whom you both feel good. You've just honored your horse's intelligence and your own intuition. Your partnership with your horse goes to a new, deeper level.

When you don't pay attention to your gut feelings with a small animal, the results may be tragic for them and emotionally hard for you. When you don't pay attention to your gut feelings with a horse, serious injury to you or to the horse can be the result. On the other hand, learning to "listen" to your horse and to trust her and your intuition can result in extraordinary, life-altering experiences. So you see, entering into a relationship with a horse is a high-stakes proposition. Are you ready to hear what your horse wants to tell you?

being

horse

chapter three

"Don't be the rider who gallops all night and never
sees the horse that is beneath him."

—Jelaluddin Rumi

The first obstacle to interspecies communication is the belief system programmed into us. Any of you who remember your parents or teachers telling you that talking with animals is impossible have accepted this belief system. Remember that other cultures have not accepted this belief system. Not only do Native and indigenous cultures believe that humans can communicate with animals, plants, and all of Nature, but they honor and respect this communication as vital to living a balanced life.

Once we believe that we can understand that our horses are communicating with us, we can begin to perceive their thoughts and feelings. You will find that believing takes effort and attention since the collective belief system exerts powerful energy in the opposite direction. It will take courage, determination, and practice to break out of the trance! Ask your horse to help you learn how to listen.

To begin connecting with your horse, observe how you approach her. As you make your way to her stable or pasture, are you thinking about her or about what you want her to do? Think about how happy you are to see her. Think about how beautiful she is. Stop and see what she's doing. Is she grazing? Is she playing with other horses? Before she notices you, stop and just look at her. Now, think about connecting to her. Don't say anything—just think about her. If she's not totally preoccupied, she'll look up and notice you. What does she do next? Does she call out to you, whinny, and come to greet you? Does she put her head down and continue to graze? What is she telling you by her response?

Make time to spend moments with your horse in a space she's comfortable in. Some horses will enjoy having you in the stall with them. They have become used to having people in the stall feeding and grooming them. However, she may be

Ask your horse to help you learn how to listen.

used to people in her stall having an agenda and not used to you just "hanging out." It may take an adjustment on her part. See if you sense her waiting for you to do something. If it's difficult for you both to just be together without doing something, it's OK to brush her and speak softly to her, telling her that you'd like to spend more time with her in order to get to know her better. Do this as often as you can until it's comfortable for you both to just be together doing nothing. Also remember that "doing nothing" for a horse usually means grazing while you linger nearby. If she's comfortable just being with you, she'll probably eat peacefully. Try to pay attention to how close she'll let you come to her, and honor her space.

Some horses will need more space in order to feel that they are free to be themselves. Observe this space. Is it the paddock or pasture? Notice at what distance your horse accepts your presence and when he feels uncomfortable. Observe your own energy. Are you calm and peaceful or are you eager and excited? A calm and peaceful attitude will be easier for your horse to accept. Now just stand and observe your horse and yourself. If you're like most of us, being still and doing nothing will be challenging. Your mind will start working. You'll start thinking about other things. Gently bring your mind back to observing your horse and your quiet connection. Each time you feel distracted by your mind or a noise, bring your awareness back to your horse and to your own breathing. Notice how your horse's sides rise and fall rhythmically. Try to breathe deeply into your belly in the same rhythmic way. This way of breathing quietly and being fully present is a way to learn how to be like a horse. With practice you will become more and more sensitive to yourself and to your horse. You can even practice when you're not with him. Sit quietly, close your eyes, and visualize your horse grazing peacefully. See yourself standing quietly nearby. Each of you is comfortable and happy in each other's presence. Breathe deeply. Think of yourself as part of your horse's herd. Feel that you belong together.

Being like your horse, even for just a few minutes a day, will facilitate and deepen the communication between the two of you. Eventually your horse will accept you as a member of her herd. This is critical to creating a relationship of trust.

GETTING STARTED

Now that you're practicing being with and like your horse, what questions would you like to ask her? I've started with the questions I have heard people ask their horses. If you look and listen deeply, the answers to these questions often hold some surprises. Feel free to pose some of these same questions to your horse. You may find that she agrees or disagrees in terms of her personal experience. Either way, you'll get to know the special individual your horse is.

relationships
with
humans

chapter four

"*Learning about our horses is learning about ourselves.*"

—Linda Tellington-Jones

What human language do you like the best?

The language of love.

A: We all respond better to a person who communicates to us with a gentle attitude and clear intent. Spoken human language is irrelevant to us. The energy and intention behind the words are what matter. We are sensitive to the energies around us. When a person with fear in his or her energy field approaches us, we usually get nervous. When a person approaches us with anger, we want to run in the opposite direction. When a person approaches us with admiration, respect, and affection, we become interested and attracted to the person.

What do you feel is the biggest communication obstacle between you and the humans in your life?

Agendas.

A: Most of you put the work/performance/riding goal first above your relationship with us. How many of you look to find a horse who can be your friend as your first priority? Most of you buy a horse because you have a goal in mind and the horse you pick is the best one to get you there. You are focusing on what the horse can do for you, not on what good friends and partners you will be to one another. This gets our relationship off track from the get-go. Choosing us for what we can do for you makes us simply a vehicle for your accomplishments. Choosing us because you care about us as an individual who can be your partner working with you toward a mutual goal would change the face of human/horse relationships for the better.

It won't take a great deal of effort on your part to make this change. It is a thought process or mind-set that depends on you being present and asking yourself, "What do I want in the perfect partnership with a horse? Is there a horse out there who wishes to be my partner? What if I choose a horse based on our connection first and on his skill level second? Won't we have a much better chance of reaching my goals if we are a team?" (The answer to the last question will be an emphatic yes from us!)

*I*s there a culture or group of people who have most closely aligned or related best to horses?

We align best with people who respect and appreciate all of our qualities.

A: Among humans there are people whose horsemanship is legendary, including cavalry officers, knights, Mongolian tribesmen, Bedouins, and Native Americans. What they have in common is an attitude that respects freedom and reveres horses. We are honored and valued highly by these people. We are loved. Riders from these cultures learned to understand a horse before asking the horse to do anything for them. They spent lots of time letting the horse get to know them before mounting and riding. They developed relationship and love before ever riding a horse. They recognized the privilege of having a horse respect them and were willing to do something with and for them. Today, good riders do not have their egos attached to us and our performance. They love and respect us as family whether we "do well" for them or not. They support and guide us into being the best we can be.

Do you distinguish between female and male guardians? Do you have a preference?

We distinguish respect versus control.

A: Of course we know the difference between male and female people. We prefer being with humans who love and respect us, who spend time being with us and loving us for who we are. We appreciate humans who are aware of our sensitivities and who value and encourage us to use our abilities to make good decisions. We admire humans who teach us how to accept and understand human environments and requirements for being together. We appreciate humans who care about our health and happiness and who provide us with a balanced living situation: time to work, play, or just be in the field. We love and admire humans who listen to us and with whom we develop and nurture mutual trust.

What specific actions can we take to help a physically abused horse regain his trust in us?

Love is the answer.

A: The first step is to give this horse unconditional love. Do not ask anything of him. Give him good, healthy food. Talk to him. Touch him wherever he'll allow you to. Put him in a pasture with horses who like and trust human beings. Ask these horses to speak with him and tell him of their experiences. Give him time. Spend as much time as you can near him or with him if possible. Always approach him with positive, loving thoughts. Never think about his pain when you're with him or feel sorry for him. See him happy and free of pain. See him playing joyfully with other horses and with you. Be his friend.

As he begins to follow you with his eyes or takes an interest in you, turn your back to him, look over your shoulder at him, smile, and begin to walk away. If he's interested in having a relationship with you, he'll follow. Stop. If he comes up to you and touches you with his nose, touch him and tell him how happy you are. Now just hang out together. When it feels right and the horse is comfortable, touch him gently and lovingly. Do this as often as you can. Later show him a halter. Ask him if he'll let you put it on him. If yes, put it on and leave it on for a short time. Ask him to follow you again. Stop and then take it off. Keep explaining to him what you wish to do and give him a few minutes to decide if he's ready for each step. Work up to adding a rope to the halter. When he's ready, take him for a walk in a place you both feel safe in. Go very slowly at introducing him to activities with humans, but do show him that he can do safe, comfortable things with a human being. If you continue to pay attention to his signals, you'll see when and where he's ready to go. Again, err on the side of moving slowly with him. If you rush or push him, you'll likely take five steps backward in your process together. Patience and love will almost always guide him back to trust.

We wish to thank all of you who have patiently helped us heal from past physical and emotional traumas. Human love is very beautiful for us to receive!

Why do horses trust their guardians, and what can we learn from this?

Our mission is to trust and to teach/engender trust.

A: When a horse accepts a human being as a partner or as the herd leader, trust is unconditional. This level of trust is earned. Some of us have higher standards than others. Some of us will trust anybody who takes charge and has a say over our food and safety. Others of us demand more. We evolve when we place our trust in humans who have earned it and continue to respect us.

Do horses like humans riding them?

That depends on our relationship with the rider.

A: We have aligned our lives with humanity for thousands of years. We have consciously agreed to accompany human beings on your physical, emotional, mental, and spiritual journeys. For many of us, we are happiest when our rider is able to consciously acknowledge how we support her in growing on all these levels. Some of us enjoy training riders to feel comfortable and confident in the saddle. Others appreciate just being friends with human beings. Many of us wish to be challenged by our riders. Some of us enjoy being ridden with skill and consideration for our physical gifts and talents. All of us want some kind of positive relationship with our rider.

Are you comfortable having more than one person ride you?

That's a matter of personal preference.

A: We are herd animals and as such enjoy a variety of relationships. The relationship between a horse and a rider is an especially intimate one. We are asked to blend ourselves with another, to carry and care for the person on our backs. This is a sacred responsibility. Some of us prefer to have this relationship with just one person in order to really develop an intimate, one-on-one connection. Others of us are happy to be ridden by anybody who appreciates us; we are born teachers and feel great satisfaction teaching many young or inexperienced riders how to ride. Relationships are all-important to us. We always seek out relationships with humans and other horses where we can grow, learn, and connect in a loving way.

Do horses know how large they are in relation to humans?

Sometimes.

A: Because we grow so fast, we are not always aware of our size in proportion to you. Some of us grow so fast we can't mentally process all of our changes. We can forget that we have a back end. We can be clumsy with our feet and sometimes bonk our heads on walls, door frames, each other, or you. Sometimes the work you train us for emphasizes our front ends too much and we lose track of our back ends. This can be dangerous for us and at the very least will lead to an imbalance in our muscles and joints—too much strength in the front and not enough in the back. If this happens, we need help to reconnect our front end to our rear end or we're bound for injuries or lameness.

It is important for you to help us know your physical boundaries and to let us know if we're not respecting your physical or energetic space. We're very sensitive to each other's space, and we will test one another to learn what the boundaries are. We will do this with you too. So let us know if we're too close for comfort and help us learn to pay attention to where we're putting our hooves and how we are moving in your space.

Some of us really love the way horses smell. *What* do we smell like to horses?

Different people smell differently.

A: Do we like human smell in general? No. On the basic level, humans smell like predators. We smell what you eat as it escapes through your pores when you sweat or are near us. A human being who is healthy and nourished smells different from one who is sick or eating non-nourishing foods. A human being who eats meat smells different from one who is a vegetarian. A human being who is gentle and loving toward us smells different from one who is pushy, aggressive, controlling, or afraid of us. It's nice to know that you love our smell. Perhaps our smell reminds you of what it's like to play in a green field and be free!

*I*f horses could tell humans one thing about how to exist in a society (large herd), what would it be?

Love one another.

A: A herd is built on individuals who love, trust, and respect one another. Because we trust one another, we share our fears and our vulnerabilities. Because each one of us respects the others, we compensate for the weaknesses of others. Because we love one another, we are always interested in supporting the best in each individual in the herd. We expect each member to express his or her strengths on the herd's behalf, and we support each member in knowing how wonderful he or she is.

horses with horses and *others*

chapter five

"*You can tell a gelding, ask a mare, but you must discuss it with a stallion.*"

—Anonymous

Do horses need to be around other horses of different ages and sexes?

Without question!

A: Horses are herd animals. This means that we have evolved and survived because we live together in family groups. Our health, happiness, and balance are based in community living. In order to be a balanced individual, each baby horse needs to learn from horses of different ages. The first important influence is his mother, then his father. It is a mistake to keep a foal away from his father—unless he is an unhappy or angry individual. Still, the foals, especially colts, need to know who their father are. As their worldview expands beyond their parents, foals must be exposed to yearlings, older mares, and geldings. It's never a good idea to isolate different age groups from one another. Keeping foals or young geldings together without exposure to mares and older horses creates tremendous social retardation and will result in inappropriate behaviors and possibly dangerous interactions once they are reunited with other horses.

What is the ideal size of a horse herd?

That depends on a variety of factors.

A: In the wild, a small herd, say five to seven horses, is easiest to protect and to feed (from a lead mare and stallion's point of view). In a domestic situation, a herd can be larger depending on the size of the pasture and the willingness of the individual horses to get along in a larger community. If the horses decide that there are too many individuals with too many personality conflicts, they will usually form comfortable smaller groups or herds within the large "herd." We're very good at choosing who we wish to be with, who complements whom, and what groupings are for every horse's highest good.

Is the stallion the leader of the herd?

Rarely.

A: Under normal circumstances, the herd is led by a mare. A mare becomes lead mare when she exhibits wisdom, physical strength or dexterity, balance, good judgment, and clear, strong communication skills. She must know and understand every member of the herd—their strengths and weaknesses. She must be decisive and gain the respect of all the members of the herd. She must also be able to act quickly when challenged by another mare or youngster and to discipline swiftly and with care so as not to cause bodily harm. This position is earned and kept as long as she can maintain her leadership qualities and balanced physical, emotional, and mental strength.

When a horse herd is under unusual duress, the stallion will take more of a leadership position. This happens when the herd is small and there is a great deal of competition for food and territory as well as frequent threats from predators, including man. Under these circumstances there is often quite a bit of sparring between stallions for mares and offspring as well as over water and/or territory.

If there is plenty of food, water, and space for the herd to live in, the stallion is more a lookout for the herd and, of course, father to the offspring. Much of the time the lead mare will have a say as to who he breeds with and when!

On a spiritual level, the stallion holds the masculine energy for the herd. If he is a balanced, wise being, these qualities will be passed onto his colts and fillies. By example, he'll foster patience, flexibility, and creativity. His herd will flow in harmony and always hold a centered balance in all activities. They will remain healthy and injury-free. His sons will learn that true strength comes from a balance of masculine and feminine energies. If he's a hot-tempered fighter, he is usually not a good father or role model as he's more interested in proving himself to everybody. His herd will lack in confidence, security, and flexibility because his fire is out of balance and always seeking a place to burn. Typically he'll overexert himself and get injured or be driven from the herd by a stronger or more balanced stallion, which the herd will prefer once they've experienced this sort of unbalanced ego.

*A*re horses of the same color similar in personality?

No, they are not.

A: Coloring is a personality statement to some extent, but it's also based on genetics. Most of us are not really that interested in what color we turn out to be. We see our colors as signs of our individuality. Sometimes our coloring works to our advantage in the wild. Sometimes we develop certain colorations to aid our survival.

When is the best time to separate a foal from his mother?

That's up to the mother.

A: The mare knows when a foal should be weaned and when he's ready to have time away from her. In a horse herd, a foal is never separated from his mother until they both are ready. Then he's never separated for good until he's ready to go out on his own as a "teenage colt." Fillies will stay with their mothers and become valuable members of their herd, usually for life. It is not appropriate for a human being to impose a weaning or a separation between mare and foal. If you do, you are being downright cruel and will create a great deal of trauma and distrust of human beings from both horses. A mother mare spends whatever time her offspring requires to help him balance in his new body. She teaches him about the earth's energies and how to circulate them through his physical and energetic bodies. She teaches him what is good to eat and where to go to be safe. She teaches him how to respect other horses, people, and boundaries. She teaches him self-control. She alone knows when he's ready for each of these lessons and when he's ready to become a contributing member of the community on his own.

What should we do when a mare rejects her foal?

This is a sad situation that can benefit from your help.

A: In the wild, the only reason a mare will reject a foal is if there is something dreadfully wrong with it and it will not be able to live on its own. In domesticated life, mares sometimes reject their healthy offspring. The reasons for this are

1. She's ill and cannot care for the foal.
2. The mare was bred against her will and was not ready to be a mother.
3. She was too young, mentally and/or emotionally.
4. She is out of balance and/or confused.
5. She has been traumatized by having previous foals taken away from her before she or they were ready.
6. She was rejected by her own mother for any of the above reasons.

If a mare rejects her foal, the most important thing you can do is get to the reason why. You must give her lots of love and attention. If you cannot get her to accept the foal within two hours, place the foal with a loving mare. Try to feed the foal by bottle under the belly of the loving mare. Talk to the mother, explain what you're doing, and never breed her again unless you are sure that she wants to be a mother. Ask the loving mare to teach the foal all he needs to know, and thank her as often as you can.

How do horses communicate with other mammals?

In many ways.

A: As prey animals, we need to be keenly aware of who is in our environment. Each horse has an energy field around her that acts like a force field, antenna, and early warning system. When we are in a herd, we link our individual energy fields together to create a globe of energy that "feels" other mammals' energy fields and their physical presence. If we identify another non-horse in our environment as friendly, such as a deer, we will reach out to them telepathically to greet them and to discuss things of importance to each of us. If we sense that an animal is unfriendly or predatory, we will first try to get a safe distance from them. We will use our body language, voices, and telepathy to frighten them if we need to. Lastly, we will use physical force if nothing else has worked.

What makes cats and horses such good friends?

We understand one another.

A: We like cats. Little cats. They understand how energy flows through all living things. Cats are sensitive to our energy fields and sometimes help us heal by working on us with their healer's techniques. They know where we're hurting and when we're out of balance. They comfort us. They enjoy living in our barns because our grains attract mice. They enjoy sharing our space and our protection. We appreciate their independence and company. They're always interesting to talk to. It is a special opportunity for us to get to know a predator. Usually we're running away from predators, but little cats pose us no threat, so we learn a lot by speaking with them. We also enjoy learning how cats work with humans to help them heal and be whole.

How do you feel about dogs?

Usually they are a challenge.

A: We tolerate dogs in our space if they are well-behaved. It is a difficult situation for each of us because we stimulate a dog's predatory or herding instinct. They stimulate our instinct for running from predators. It always takes a great deal of self-control for a horse and dog to get along. We can become friends only when each of us is mentally and emotionally mature or evolved enough to get past the instincts.

*I*s it hard for you to see cats and dogs come inside with us while you have to stay outside?

That depends on our relationships.

A: When we feel very close to the humans in our lives we do sometimes wish we could be with you wherever you are. Herd animals have a strong instinct to remain in visual and energetic contact with other members of our herd. It is unnatural and stressful to be separated from fellow herd members. It is difficult for a horse to be alone. If you are our only herd member, it is stressful for us when you go inside the house and leave us outside. If we consider the family dogs and cats part of our herd, then we'll miss them too. If we are in the company of other horses, we will turn to them for comfort and learn to accept that you go away sometimes. It's also helpful if a cat or two lives with us in the barn or at least spends some time with us there.

caring
for body and mind

chapter six

"*Horses and children, I often think, have a lot
of the good sense there is in the world.*"

—Josephine Demott Robinson

What do you need to eat?

*A variety of healthy grasses,
herbs, and some grains.*

A: Because we are herbivores and grazers, we excel at choosing the grasses and herbs we need to stay healthy. Our very survival as a species has depended on a keen awareness of what we need to eat. However, we need sufficient territory and grass varieties in order to choose the best for us. If we are not pastured in a large pasture with lots of different grasses and herbs, we need you to help us by providing a balanced diet. Please be careful what you feed us. Since most of us can't choose our own foods, we depend on you to pay attention to the ingredients. We need more than "sweet feeds" or alfalfa hay. Grains with molasses or other refined sugars are terrible for us. Too much sugar breaks down our immune systems, just like it does to human immune systems. Hay by itself creates digestive problems. We can't digest corn or a lot of wheat. Processed pellets are not easy for us to digest. Chemicals and pesticides on grass and in grain feeds are killing us slowly and surely. A variety of healthy, balanced grass is essential for us. Our digestive systems are not terribly efficient, and most of us are not in great shape nutritionally. If we are not living in healthy pastures, we need supplementation, but it must be food source—fresh or freshly dried herbs and food-based vitamins—in order for our bodies to be able to utilize them. Young foals and old horses need help breaking down the nutrients in food. We must have the right balance of healthy bacteria in our guts in order to do this. Young bodies may be underdeveloped in this area—especially if the foal has been weaned too soon. Old bodies are "worn out" from working so hard to digest correctly. Supplementing us with this healthy bacteria can be very helpful and is becoming more and more necessary as life-force energy and healthy bacteria are depleted from soils. If it's not in the soil, it won't be in the plants.

Please pay attention to our age and activity levels when you feed us. Hardworking or performing horses need extra proteins and fats to support them. Our teeth get worn as we age, so please look in our mouths from time to time to be sure our teeth are healthy.

How do you feel about vaccinations and drugs?

Terrible!

A: The quantity of vaccines and drugs we are given is breaking down our immune systems instead of building them up. Nature exposes us to an illness; we either develop the antibodies or we die. If we survive an illness, we are stronger for being exposed to it and we'll pass this on to our offspring. If we develop the antibodies, we have them for life unless we get really run down and have nothing left of our immune systems. If we have the antibodies, why give us another dose of a vaccine? Over-drugging us makes no sense and is weakening us as a species. Steroids, antibiotics, and anti-inflammatory drugs do not heal us. They may mitigate symptoms for a time, which gives us the opportunity to heal, but they are not doing the healing.

Surgery, medicine, and other therapies should not be used to keep a horse performing when he needs to rest his body, to have his workload reduced, or to retire. Some of us will push ourselves beyond our physical limits, often because this quality has been bred into us. If you care about us, help us slow down and learn to accept retirement if our bodies are worn out.

How do you feel about herbal medicines, acupuncture, and chiropractic and energetic forms of healing?

Much better!

A: The first thing is to understand that the only true healing is reminding a horse of perfect health and balance. Holistic forms of healing are better "reminders" since they strengthen our systems. Herbal remedies and medicines are ideally suited to us since we are herbivores. The fresher, the better. We have a natural affinity for acupuncture because it addresses our intricate energy systems and helps unclog blocked energies as well as helping to rebalance and redirect the flow of energies through our bodies. When we have pain and inflammation, it's important to get to the cause before treating it. It's important to use herbs, acupuncture, massage, chiropractic, and other non-invasive therapies in order to stimulate our body's own inner healing abilities. Less stress will help us remain healthier. The best medicine for us is this:

1. Fresh air, sunshine, and a pasture to run in
2. Healthy, chemical-free food
3. Rest and herbs if we're out of balance
4. Love and touch

Have horses throughout time always foundered?

Not always.

A: Founder is a symptom of captivity. Hard floors, cement, dark stalls, inappropriate foods and/or not enough variety are its causes. Stress and unhappiness are also factors.

Grey horses aren't born grey. They develop into grey and seem to be prone to melanoma. Is there a reason for this?

Skin cancers are on the rise.

A: Grey horses and white-faced horses of any color combination are more susceptible to skin cancers. We have always been grey and white-faced. Cancer is a manifestation of imbalance in the air, land, water, plants, mammals, and humans. Humans have created this imbalance in the environment, and it's up to you to change the mind-set and thoughts that have contributed to it. Cancer is caused by a feeling of separation. Separation causes diseases of the body, heart, and mind. When you see other humans as enemies, you are in separation and are contributing to disease. Angry, fearful, and self-centered thoughts begin a dangerous chain of events that result in pollution and cancer. When you see that we are all connected, you will begin to heal. When you see the earth as an extension of yourselves as well as your source of life in form, the earth and all her inhabitants will heal.

How do stallions feel about being gelded?

That depends on the stallion and their mission with horses and with humanity.

A: In the wild, a stallion must be a stallion. Over the thousands of years that horses have been with humans, we have learned that castration goes with the territory. Sometimes castration is acceptable and even desirable when the horse understands how it will help him be able to work more with human beings. Geldings do not have the same intense hormonal fluctuations and urges to procreate that stallions do. They are able to focus primarily on their "job" with humans as a top priority since their stallion days are over.

Most of the time, however, we're castrated out of fear that we will become unmanageable if we remain intact. Sometimes this can be true. Humans often breed us for the very temperaments that would not be desired by us in the wild, such as a fiery temper. A hot-tempered stallion is a stallion out of balance in a wild horse herd. In our natural environment, a fiery colt would be strongly disciplined by the lead mare and guided to find his balance. However, in our lives with humans this is not usually the case. On one hand, human ego, especially male ego, is stimulated by a fiery stallion. Male humans have seen such stallions as a reflection of their own powerful "unbridled" masculine sexuality and have sought to both own and control this "beast." They have both fear and admiration for the physical power of a hot stallion. So humans like to breed us to exhibit these qualities that reflect back on themselves and then find a way to control us for the behaviors they've deliberately encouraged. This makes little sense to us.

The result of years of breeding stallions with hot tempers is that most people believe that a colt remaining intact will be unmanageable at best and potentially dangerous at worst. Stallions used for breeding often lead difficult lives separated from their herds or living in small, cramped spaces. Remember, separation is the most unnatural state for us and creates tension and stress. If stallions are not allowed to mount the mares naturally, they must suffer the further humiliation of being "milked" for artificial insemination. This is a poor quality of life. A stallion forced to live in these conditions will become depressed and disengaged from life. His sperm will lack life-force energy because of his lack of joy. Ultimately, his offspring will be unhealthy shadows of what a horse should be.

So if you are considering gelding your colt, we suggest that you ask yourself these questions:

1. Are you doing this because he has exhibited uncontrollable tendencies?

2. Are you doing this because you've been told this is the way it needs to be?
3. Have you talked to him about it?
4. Have you explained how the procedure is done?
5. Have you explained what your work together will be and why you feel he'll do better at it as a gelding?
6. Have you given him time to energetically, mentally, emotionally, and physically prepare for the procedure?
7. Have you given him a chance to show you that he can do what you ask of him as a balanced stallion?

When you take the time to think about these questions yourself and to give your colt time to think as well, you'll make a thoughtful decision. Your colt will have time to prepare and will deeply appreciate your respectful consideration of his point of view.

A stallion in balance has the ability to make decisive moves and to handle challenging decisions and/or situations with courage and full-hearted commitment. But it's up to the rider to examine his or her own balance, self-control, focus, and strength—mental and emotional as well as physical—to determine if a stallion is the right match. Balanced strength on all levels, not ego, is the key here.

How do you feel about artificial insemination?

Natural selection comes from a higher power than human selection.

A: A mare must agree to and accept a stallion. The act of procreation is a sacred dance. For the offspring to be healthy and whole on all levels, there must be the sacred dance between the mother and father. In this sacred dance, two consenting partners merge their energies to welcome the spirit of another horse into the mother and to create a body for this spirit who will be the best of both parents. This is always our intention in coupling. Mare and stallion are cooperating for the highest good of our herd, our breed, and our species. This is our divine right and responsibility, just as it is yours. Many mares who absorb their fetuses or reject their newborn foals are doing this because they've been artificially inseminated or mounted against their will.

We recognize that you will not abandon artificial insemination overnight. But we implore you to decide to do it only if you are deeply committed to your mare and to speaking to her about the stallion whose sperm you are asking her to accept. Be sure that the stallion is happy and balanced—not isolated and alone. If you really care about the mare and the foal you are now helping to be conceived, give her the choice to accept artificial insemination or not. Accept that by interceding in this intimate situation you have even more responsibility toward the offspring. Understand that you are contributing to an unnatural situation and do your best to offset this major negative with love and care for the horses involved.

Why do you switch your tails?

We switch our tails for many reasons.

A: Our tails are our natural fly agitators, as you can see, but we also use our tails to express different feelings to one another. As a rule, a tail carried to the right can mean that we are uncomfortable with someone. A tail carried to the left means that we are getting angry. Some of us switch our tails back and forth like cats do when we're angry, nervous, or irritated. When we're walking or grazing, we often swing our tails rhythmically from side to side to calm ourselves or the horses around and behind us. Some of us develop our own tail language if we cannot use our mouths and faces because of heavy-duty bits and bridles. Our tails show whether we are tense or relaxed. Some of us who have not been normally socialized with other horses do not know how to read another horse's tail. We have to learn. Those of us who hold a lot of tension in our tails often benefit from gentle pulling and partial rotating of our tails—if we feel comfortable and trust the person doing it! Some of us—Arabians, for example—raise our tails as a sign of excitement and to show how beautiful we are. Don't you wish you had a tail?

How do you feel if we cut or braid your tails?

Cutting our tails severely limits our ability to express our feelings to one another.

A: It separates us from one of our natural and necessary means of communication. Braiding our tails at the top is acceptable, as long as we can use the tail when we need to. Ask yourself why you feel you have to cut or coif our tails. We'd rather have you brush and appreciate our tails for the wonderful appendages they are than to impose restrictions on them and us.

What about cutting or braiding your manes?

Cutting or braiding our manes is not so invasive for us.

A: Some of us who naturally grow long, luxurious manes feel naked and vulnerable without them. Some of us who live in harsh climates with lots of sand, rain, or snow need our manes to protect our eyes and faces.

Do horses need to gallop every day?

Yes, most of us do.

A: No horse is happy or healthy if only allowed to move in controlled or limited ways. Our bodies are designed to move in different ways. In fact, our health depends on our movement. Fluid movement is critical to our well-being. We must be allowed the space and time to explore how our bodies move through air and in contact with the earth. It is essential for young horses to explore all varieties of movement. They must learn how to lie down, roll, get up, walk, trot, canter, gallop, twist, turn, buck, and jump. Each different movement stimulates the muscles, bones, joints, and mind differently. It is critical for our development to experience all types of movement—on our own and in our own timing, not just when humans want us to.

Horses who are forced to perform in limited ranges of motion day after day—dressage horses or trotters, for example—are destined for physical, emotional, and mental difficulties. They must receive time and space to explore other types of movements or they will become unbalanced.

Do horses need to move on different types of terrain?

Absolutely.

A: When we are exposed only to smooth trails or sandy arenas, our hooves suffer. For our hooves and legs to stay healthy and strong, we need to move on dry and wet earth, rocks, stones, grass, sand, and hard roads, in rain or shine. If we live where it's cold, we need to learn how to handle ice and snow beneath our hooves. Exposing us to a variety of terrain also helps us mentally as we learn how to balance our bodies under different conditions. Again, variety stimulates us. When we learn how to handle different situations, we become more accepting, relaxed, and able to cope with changes of any sort.

How do horses navigate and move so fast over uneven terrain?

We read the air and the earth.

A: Our hooves, specifically the tender area you refer to as the "frog," has the ability to read the electromagnetic pulses of the earth we walk or run on. We absorb the earth's energies into our hooves, up our legs, and into our bodies, and then we circulate it back down into the earth—all in the blink of an eye. It is imperative for our health that we have this connection. Many hoof, leg, and circulation problems develop in horses who are confined to stalls or on cement all the time because they are not able to have this energetic flow of information from earth to body and back again. We also read the air by smelling and sensing electromagnetic changes in the atmosphere. We feel these changes as they pass over and through our very sensitive energy fields, just as you feel a wave of heat or a cold breeze pass over your skin. We use all our sensitivities to navigate. We rely on our mental memories or on the mental memories of herd members as well as on our cellular memories to help us remember where to find water, safe haven, and specific meadows with specific medicinal herbs. Just like water, we seek the path of least resistance. We listen to the earth, and she always tells us what we need to know.

How do you feel about horseshoes?

We've grown accustomed to them, but...

A: Most of us have lifetimes of memories of wearing horse-shoes. Horseshoes were developed for horses who spent their lives working daily on human roads. Humans learned that horses' hooves wear down when exposed day in and day out to those hard roads. In order to preserve our hooves, you invented iron shoes. Shoes are helpful if we are working on hard roads every day. However, they are not necessary if we are pastured, working in sandy arenas, or walking on earth trails. In those cases shoes provide an unnecessary barrier between our hooves and the earth.

Each horse's hooves are different, just as all human feet are different. Shoes that are comfortable for some of us are not comfortable for others. Some shoes distort our legs and backs; some shoes help compensate for hoof, leg, or back problems. Again, each horse's four feet, build, type of work, and individual balance need to be taken into consideration when choosing shoes. Nails are an old-fashioned and often damaging way of attaching shoes to horse hooves and should be replaced with kinder, gentler alternatives. If shoes must be worn for our activity and our own protection, we ask that you give our hooves the attention needed to keep them healthy so we can continue to be happy and sound.

Overall, it's healthier for horses to learn how to be without shoes if they are not working on hard surfaces every day or living in very wet or very dry climates. Our hooves are strong and tough if our bodies are receiving healthy food and a variety of exercises. Think about leaving the hooves of foals naked so that they can develop the right toughness in their hooves. If a horse is encouraged to be shoeless, and is comfortable without shoes, he'll be more balanced and healthy. Standing on one's own four feet in contact with the earth is how we're built to be.

Is your equipment (tack) comfortable?

Most equipment was designed to make humans more comfortable or in better control.

A: All tack and equipment such as saddles, bridles, and bits were designed by you to make riding or driving us easier for you. None of it was designed just for us. Some equipment helps us in certain situations, but as a rule, less is more. What we mean by this is that the less a person depends on their equipment, the more they depend on us.

Western saddles are like chairs on our backs. Of course this helped the cowboy stay on when we executed difficult moves together herding cows and it helped support him when he had to ride us for long hours. But a Western saddle is not comfortable for us to wear. We can get used to them, of course, but they are far from natural for us. Like shoes create a barrier between us and the earth, saddles create a barrier between us and our riders. An English saddle is better since there's less leather between the two of us. It is more flexible and moves better with our bodies. When riders use less equipment they have to use more of their bodies to "hold on" to our bodies. There is a better connection. When a saddle must be used, it is important that it fit each of us correctly. One size does not fit all; saddles must be individually sized. This can't be done long-distance. The saddlemaker must see us, measure us, and know where our individual pressure points are. If this attention is not paid to our body, you can be sure our saddle will be uncomfortable. And we cannot harmonize properly with our rider if we are constantly distracted by our equipment.

Girths are just plain irritating. Think of a girth as a tight belt holding a chair on your back. The belt has to be pretty tight to hold the chair in the right place. It also compresses us where we need to expand our diaphragms in order to breathe deeply. You get the idea. Again, we have gotten used to them because we've had to. Halters are OK but shouldn't be left on all the time. Bits of all kinds are very unpleasant. We would be much happier without them.

Bridles, reins, and bits become unnecessary when horse and rider trust one another and are connected heart, body, and mind. In other words, you don't have to pull our heads to direct us but rather use your thoughts to direct us and also trust us to move with you in the appropriate direction. To develop your physical strength to ride without a saddle and your mental strength to ride without a bit or reins, you need to spend a lot of time with us. For us to develop a telepathic connection, you have to be with us and practice. This is relationship!

We appreciate that reins, bits, and bridles are necessary when we have to do challenging things on a busy roadway with cars, bicycles, and other "unnatural" things around to frighten us. We have accepted that your equipment allows you to feel safe with us and helps you learn how to ride us. We are stating here that we long for greater connection with you. Again, one of the best ways for this to happen is for you to have less equipment to rely on so you have to be in greater physical and mental contact with us. When you do this, we can both enjoy an intimate relationship that does not hinder comfortable movement.

Why do horses snort?

To clear our noses.

A: We snort to clear our noses of dust and dirt and to clear the dust or dirt off of plants we wish to eat. Sometimes we snort in greeting. We snort/sigh when we need to relax or to tell another horse that it's OK to relax.

How do you feel about being left outside in the weather and with potential predators?

This is our natural state.

A: It is unnatural for us to be inside every day or night. We feel most at home in a field where we can smell the changes in the weather, smell predators, and deal with the natural rhythm of life. Being exposed to different weather conditions helps us learn to pay attention to subtle atmospheric changes. Living in rain and sleet can strengthen our minds because we need to think about how to stay warm, how to support one another in the herd, and how to protect the foals or others inexperienced with weather changes—those who have grown up in stables and barns and now are out to pasture. Being exposed to weather changes strengthens our bodies as it helps our hooves and coats. All of these benefits depend on our healthy state of body and mind. A sick horse will be challenged by changing weather conditions and will need nutritional or other support from humans caring for him. If we live in places of extreme weather conditions, we appreciate having a shelter to go to if we need to.

Dealing with predators is a thing we are built to do. We have never forgotten that we are prey animals and sometimes need to give ourselves to a predator. This is part of life.

How does it affect you when we transport you into climates you did not develop in?

It's a challenge.

A: Those of us who developed in the desert do not have the body fat, hooves, or coats to be really comfortable in cold, wet climates. Those of us who developed in cold, windy, rocky places are not comfortable in hot, dry, sandy places. All of us can do well in temperate climates.

As a horseman, *how* can I do a better job of nurturing and taking care of my horse?

Pay attention, stay in your heart, and communicate!

A: The first thing to determine is whether or not you have the time to spend with us. Once a week or a couple of hours a couple of times a week will not be enough to co-create a strong relationship. Relationship is everything. We cannot have a partnership with you if you don't spend time just being with us. When you're with us, really be with us. If you're talking to people or thinking about other things, you are not being present with us. We can feel this separation and are unhappy around you. If you are really present with us, talk to us and touch us. Just hang out with us. This builds relationship.

Next, pay attention to our food, shelter, and environment. Is there enough space for us to run and play? Are we getting the nutrients we need? Is our shelter clean and dry? Are you happy in the work or play we do together? If we have a trainer, do you trust this person? Did the trainer sit and talk with you before we began working with him, asking you what you and I want to accomplish together? Does he repeatedly ask you if you and I are enjoying the training? Does he help you pay attention to my comfort and confidence as well as your own? Is he supporting us to grow together or is he imposing his own agenda? You nurture us best when you, our rider/guardian, are in charge. When you are leading the trainer and us, we feel supported and in your care as herd leader. This is the best way to take care of us.

Do horses mind being confined in stalls?

We are designed to live in open spaces.

A: It is very difficult for us to spend many hours in a stall. How would you like to be left in a small, cramped, usually dark space? We are designed to live in open spaces, to feel the wind, to be able to run and play whenever the mood hits us. After hundreds of years, we've learned to accept being in stalls for periods of time. Some of us feel safe with our three walls. Many of us can accept being in a stall sometimes. All of us need to balance stall time with pasture time. If you know a horse who is unhappy in the pasture, it's because he has only known confinement. He must be reeducated to accept freedom and its responsibilities.

What do horses need for a good life at home?

We need relationships.

A: We are social beings. Our entire sense of security, stability, orientation, and self depends on our relationships. We need to know how we "fit" with others. We need to feel friendship, love, cooperation, and personal challenges. We need to really know other horses and people. The more familiar we are with other horses, people, places, and things, the more comfortable we are. Our ability to handle new experiences is directly proportional to how many relationships we've been exposed to. If a young horse is exposed to other horses, different stalls, new arenas and trails, strange people, and different equipment, the more he's able to cope with change and the more cooperative he'll be when asked to do something new or challenging. Exposing a horse to different experiences is vital for his mental, emotional, and physical development.

In order for us to be happy, we also need to be understood as individuals. We need respect. We need patience and gentleness. We need boundaries. And we need to be asked to do things. If people think to ask us to cooperate, to work together with them on a shared goal, we're extremely happy because then the relationship has become a partnership.

What do you need for a good life in the wild?

Relationships.

A: Our relationships are the foundations of our survival in the wild. Our herd, our family, is our safety and our refuge. Without a wise lead mare and a strong stallion, we are extremely vulnerable. When we have a herd bound by love and respect, we are not afraid of anything except separation. Separation is the only thing we fear.

We also need freedom to be ourselves, freedom to find healing foods and water, and freedom to play and to run.

How do you cope with being sold and moved?

*It's all in how we're prepared
for the change.*

A: Because we are herd animals, we expect that we will live in a community for our entire lives. Male horses expect to leave their mother and father's herd and move on to create their own. Female horses expect to stay in their mother's herd.

That said, we have learned through living and working with human beings for centuries that we cannot expect our lives to always follow our natural rhythms. If we have a close bond with a human who must sell us, it's very important that we have time together before we are separated and that you explain where and to whom we are going. We need time to say good-bye to the horses we've lived with and time to prepare for the change—at least two days, hopefully a week.

Once we are in the new home, it's imperative for us to find other horses and/or humans to bond with. We'll need time to be accepted into the new herd and to get used to the new environment. Familiar activities, equipment, food, and smells are reassuring to us and help us accept our new home.

horse on *performing* and competing

chapter seven

"*A man on a horse is spiritually as well as physically bigger than a man on foot.*"

—John Steinbeck

How can I best prepare you for a long trail ride?

Talk to us.

A: Many of you talk about us, not to us. Why do you do this? We understand most of what you say when you take the time to really speak to us. So first, tell us about the ride you'd like us to carry you on. Be sure that we're interested in listening to you and in good physical and mental shape to do the ride today. If you were going on a long hike with human friends, you'd ask them how they feel about a particular trail. You'd ask them what they planned to bring if you needed to eat together. You'd be sure that there was enough water available for you both. During the hike you'd pay attention to their comfort level, and if they appeared uncomfortable you'd ask them if they'd like to rest. We would appreciate the same considerations.

How do thoroughbreds feel about racing?

Usually this life is very difficult.

A: Thoroughbreds are built for speed and to enjoy running. For hundreds of years we have loved racing as much as you have loved to watch us. However, two-year-olds are not physically, emotionally, or mentally ready for grueling racing schedules. If a youngster really loves to run, he or she may become a "champion" as long as no injuries occur. A two-year-old is more prone to injury than a four-year-old, because an older horse has better self-control and body awareness, and their tendons, ligaments, muscles, bones, and joints are developed enough to race. A two-year-old has not the mental or physical maturity to race on humans' schedules. The racing circuit is full of abuse and mistreatment for the majority of horses. The thrill of watching us run has become all about money, not about us. Most horses bred to race do not become "champions." If we're lucky, we end up in a kind home.

A few years ago there was a phenomenon on the Kentucky racing farms. An alarming number of foals died.

Other mares absorbed fetuses. Humans tried to blame it on disease and "bad grass." This was far from the truth. We were making a statement. The mares needed to send a message that they didn't wish to bring foals into the abusive world of racing anymore. We were trying to get your attention. Some of you understood, but not enough of you.

Only humans can return horse racing to an activity that honors the equine athlete by putting his well-being above all else. When this happens, we will feel that our relationship with humanity has really blossomed into something beautiful.

How do you feel about rodeos?

They are very stressful and often frightening.

A: When rodeos started, horses and cows were treated with care and respect because they were the valuable property of the ranchers and cowboys who created rodeo. Rodeo was a way to showcase a cowboy's rapport and skill with his horse and to some extent with the cows. Again, the horses and cows were the men's livelihood. The men never wished to harm a horse or cow. Sadly, the competition has now taken precedence over the well-being of the horses and cows. In present-day rodeos, every animal is under tremendous physical and emotional stress, and many are often injured and killed. We are being used for the glory and thrill humans get from competing. This saddens us tremendously. Occasionally some of us will enjoy barrel racing or cutting, but we are always aware of our fellow animals who are miserable.

How do you feel about pulling carriages in cities?

It's grueling work.

A: The hardest thing about pulling carriages is the asphalt and the temperatures, and after that, the pollution and the noise. If we have good shoes, built to support us on asphalt, this helps. If we do not work in the heat of the day or at peak traffic times, we can manage. Some of us actually enjoy the attention we receive and like to work. To survive as carriage horses, we need a balance of days on and days off and to feel soft earth under our feet when we're "off duty." We also need to be mentally well-suited for the job and to be with human beings who pay attention to our stress levels and care about our well-being.

How do you feel about
performing in circuses?

That depends on how all the
animals are being treated.

A: We enjoy performing when we love and care for the person who teaches us to perform and when we are appreciated by the audience for our efforts and talents. If the other animals in the circus are unhappy or mistreated, though, we pick up on that and feel unhappy as well. We do not wish to be seen just as objects of entertainment. We are living, breathing beings who think and feel. If some of us choose to entertain, that's our individual choice, just as it is up to you to choose whether or not you wish to be an entertainer. We ask you to look carefully to see whether we're happy performing. If we are happy, you will feel uplifted. If we're unhappy, you'll feel differently.

What about other forms of performing—dressage, jumping, eventing, and endurance rides?

We love to participate with partners in balanced competitions.

A: Each of us is suited to a particular form of exercise. We have agreed to be bred for characteristics that suit us to certain athletic and working disciplines. Some of us love dressage but will get in trouble if we are not provided with free periods to play and stretch after hours of controlled, precise exercises. Many of us love to jump, but we must have mental and physical balance as well as a sense of taking care of our riders. Partnership is essential in jumping and in eventing. You need us to think and be able to make good decisions because you can't possibly carry this responsibility all the time. The greater the physical and mental challenge, the more critical it is that horse and rider are mental and physical equals and partners so that one can take over when the other falters. The "secret" of every great horse-and-rider team is this deep understanding of partnership.

Endurance rides can be fun and challenging, but they are fun only if you pay attention to our need for rest. Remember, we want to do these things when we're in connection and partnership with you. Anything not in partnership is disappointing and unfulfilling—for us both, whether you consciously realize it or not.

the *spiritual* side of life

chapter eight

"When a woman spends time around a horse, she finds
a flesh-and-blood Muse to sing to her soul."
—Mary Midkiff from *She Flies Without Wings*

Do you perceive other animals and humans as conscious beings with individual differences?

Absolutely!

A: We are very sensitive to the information carried in the energy field of individual humans as well as individual animals and herds or packs of animals. We can easily perceive an individual's level of awareness or consciousness.

Some horses reach out and touch our hearts, while others seem to ignore us. *A*re horse souls at different levels of awareness?

Yes, just as with humans.

A: Many of us have been with human beings for thousands of lifetimes. We have evolved as individuated souls and can choose to come back to teach and to serve God/Life. Others of us are earlier on in our development as souls. Those of us who are not as experienced bonding with humans usually are intimate only with other horses. Each horse soul is growing and evolving as each human soul is. Often horse souls and human souls bond and reincarnate together. There will always be a deep connection between these souls.

There are different reasons for us to make deep connections with human beings. There are different reasons for why we "ignore" human beings. One is that we have learned that it's safer for us to remain detached and to look out for ourselves since we are forced to live and work around and with human beings who are not really interested in our safety or happiness. This can protect us physically and emotionally from certain kinds of abuse and neglect. A second reason is that no person has taken the time to develop a relationship with us. You're too busy "working" us to really know and love us.

Some of us reach out and make a great effort to connect to our humans because we want a real relationship. This means that we have to open our hearts and show our person that we want to connect to them. A horse who has succeeded at having a good relationship with a human in one lifetime is likely to strive for that in his subsequent lifetimes. We carry the quality of idealism. Once we have felt and reciprocated love with a human being, we will strive to achieve it again and again.

What would the horse council consider to be the ultimate achievement for a horse?

Balance.

A: We are here to learn and to teach balance in all things. This means that we strive for physical, emotional, mental, and spiritual balance all the time. We remember past life-times and always seek to rebalance or to create better balance for ourselves lifetime to lifetime. Through our relationship with humans, we also seek balance. We seek health and physical balance. We seek a balance between doing and being. We seek to be in balance with all life on the planet. We need to move in balance and teach our riders to ride with balance on all levels. If we can accomplish our own balance and help other horses or humans find theirs, then we've contributed to planetary balance.

What happens when you die?

We go to the Place of Reunification.

A: All of us go to the same "place" when we pass out of form. Our spirits return to the "sea" of all Life. We return to God, to Light, to Love. As we pass into the Light, we try to leave behind any destructive experiences and seek balance by recalibrating to the Light. Some of us are more successful at this than others. Traumatic deaths are difficult to shed. Disconnected, painful lives are difficult to forget. We often carry these memories through many lifetimes, repeating traumas and getting stuck in destructive patterns—just as human beings do. Often we return to specific humans who we know will help us heal and return to balance. Loving humans who respect us and listen to us can help free us of painful memories. We are deeply grateful for your help when you give it. Often a human and a horse help each other release past traumas.

It is the gift/duty of every being who knows love to shine their loving light so that others may gravitate toward it and be healed. No being really heals another; they just provide a well of love for another soul to dip into so they can find themselves and be whole again.

Do individual horse spirits linger near people they love?

Sometimes.

A: If we love a person or other horses, we may choose to check in with them after we have left our bodies. It is best for us to die without pain or trauma (injections—never bullets, please—if you have to help us die). We can then pass quickly into the Light to be restored, and after that return in spirit if we choose to. All beings should be sent to the Light with love. If we are sent with sadness, fear, anger, or pain, we may get stuck in between the world of form and the world of Light. If you feel a horse friend lingering in the between, please encourage him to go to God. Say a prayer or do a ceremony to help him go. This will usually work unless he has some unfinished business to attend to.

If we choose to return to you in spirit, know that we are doing this out of love and wish you to know that we want to support you in living your life in balance and love. We can become helping angels, so to speak, if you're open to our being with you in this way.

How do individual horses decide to return in a new body to the person they loved?

Just like humans do.

A: As individuated souls, we have free choice to return to horses and/or to humans we have loved. We decide to do this when we feel that it is in everybody's highest or best interest at a soul level. We do this when we have something more to learn or to teach or if we feel we can help other horse or human souls achieve greater levels of balance and love. There are "master teachers" in horse bodies, just as there are in human bodies.

Do you see and feel energy?

Absolutely!

A: As prey animals, we are keenly aware of the energies around us. We feel it, smell it, sense it in our own energy fields and in our bodies, and sometimes even taste it. We transfer this ability to "feeling" our human beings. We read your energies, intentions, state of health, and balance. Often when we are in a close, caring relationship with you, we feel your imbalances before you're aware of them. We are acutely aware of negative or harmful energies pointed in our direction. We're also just as aware of loving, positive energies.

Do horses have angels?

Yes.

A: Each horse has a guide or guardian angel. Some of us have more than one. A guide may be a horse spirit or a human spirit. Some of us are more aware of our guides than others. A guardian angel is always a being from the Angelic Realm. The Angelic Presence who watches over all horses is often called the "over-lighting" Angel of Equines.

Can horse guides serve to guide humans?

Of course!

A: When a horse who loves a human passes out of form, this horse will usually watch over that human throughout her lifetime. If the person works with other horses, the horse guide can help from the spirit realm. In other words, if you would like the beloved deceased horse's help with training or healing horses in form, you have only to ask. Our spirits are eternal, and when love has connected us with a human being, we are always willing to guide and support that human throughout her life.

Do horses have a pre-life contract to come onto the earth to serve a role or special purpose?

We always have a purpose in coming into form.

A: Just as every human being does, each horse comes into form to grow and to learn. Although many humans at this time are unconscious of their individual soul's purpose, horses always have a conscious sense of why they are in form. Some of us come to serve and to teach, but this is always a learning process as well. If we have lived a painful lifetime, we will usually return to heal those memories. Sometimes the memories are so traumatic that we get stuck and repeat them over and over again. You do this as well. All souls and all beings in form have a desire to return to balance, wholeness, happiness, and love. This is our greatest purpose. We all share this.

At this moment in time, Master Teacher horses are reincarnating. We are coming to reestablish and anchor the original contract of love and mutual respect between equines and humans. We feel that there is a shift taking place in human consciousness, and we are here to support it. These Master Teachers work on the energetic planes to cleanse, heal, balance, and realign all the energies in their environment. They are helping to heal the planet. Each human who believes that this is possible can support us by staying in their hearts and by giving energy to love and connection—not to fear and separation. This is of critical importance at this moment in time. Every human alive today is being asked to choose Love over fear. This decision starts with the little choices in everyday life, which leads to clarity with the bigger choices.

*I*s there a horse god?

No, there is not a separate god for us or for any living being.

A: God is the god of all creatures. There is one Source for all people, animals, plants, and rocks. You may call this being by different names, but He/She is One. She/He is Love.

Do horses dream? If so, what do you dream about?

Yes, we dream about many things, just as you do.

A: We dream of joyful things and we have nightmares about traumatic or frightening things. We do not really have a "subconscious" mind because we are fully aware beings. Many of you hold traumas in your subconscious mind in order to protect yourselves. We can't do that, so our past traumas, whether in this lifetime or in an earlier one, are present in our conscious minds. You see this in horses who are terrified of something they've "never" seen before. Often they are remembering the terror from another lifetime, or something has reminded them of a frightening experience. This may appear to you as if we have astounding memories. The fact is that you have the same ability to remember past-life traumas as well, but you just tend to stuff them into your "subconscious" mind. Eventually these nightmares will need to be addressed and healed. We always seek out the healing and try to cooperate with anybody who tries to help us. Do you?

Do horses have soul mates?

We are all soul mates.

A: As herd animals, we have a deep connection to one another. When we live in the wild, some of us choose to reincarnate with a beloved mate lifetime after lifetime. We do this if it is for the highest good of our family herd and if we're contributing to the improvement of our species. In domesticated life, we tend to focus more on our relationships with humans. However, some "soul mate" horses will reincarnate into domesticity in order to help the humans they love understand and appreciate horse love. Some horse soul mates are incarnating now into domesticity in order to infuse and remind all horses of this sacred relationship and to bring into form Master Teacher offspring to help guide humanity back into connection with all life forms.

How are you serving mankind other than in the daily work you do for us?

We do not serve mankind.

A: We serve God. We help human beings on their path to reunification with all creatures on the earth, but we are not your servants. When you see us as servers to humankind you completely miss the point of our relationship with you. No being on this planet is subservient to another. The fact that humans could ever perceive of another human, animal, or plant as a servant simply indicates the large degree of disconnection some humans have. We all are one—different aspects or expressions of the Divine One. We are here to help you remember this and to teach you love and trust so that you can share this with other humans and non-humans.

In this time of great changes in life on earth, is there any thing the council of equines would like us to know?

Love will survive.

A: Each and every human is now being offered the chance to choose love over fear every minute of every day. Love is inclusive. It is your natural state, even though so many of you seem overpowered by fear at this time. Do not lose hope. Give your thoughts and energies to love—not to approval, which is based in a fear of not being loved, but to true love. True love has no criteria. It is based on acceptance and right action. Use your hearts more and your minds less. Your very survival depends on you learning to tell the difference. You must learn to listen to that which strengthens the heart and connects you to your human brothers and sisters and to your non-human sisters and brothers. You are made of the same stuff that all of us are made of. Remember that. We are all one. We believe in you. We trust that you will return to Love.

in the company *of Horses*

This book has been a labor of love—for all the horses I've met and for all the people who have ever loved or been loved by a horse. The magnificent equine enriches our lives in countless ways. Living with horses provides us a glimpse into an extraordinary community whose lives depend on balanced relationships and supporting one another. It is my dream that horse people will rekindle the ancient partnership and learn to honor their horses as they would respected friends. As I re-read the horses' answers to our questions and insights, I get something new each time. Amazing beings.

Here is what the Council of Horses has to say to you:

"We are Family. Always remember this. We tread this path called life together, and if we learn to listen carefully to one another, our lives will be enriched, our souls will expand and all will be balanced in the world. Let us carry you to God. Love and cherish us. Understand that we come in Friendship and Trust us. Together we are greater than the sum of our parts."

May you return to this book over and over as you journey through your life in the company of horses.

about

the Author

K ATE S OLISTI -M ATTELON, internationally-known speaker, author and teacher, is a professional animal communicator. Since 1992, she has worked with individual animal guardians, holistic veterinarians, trainers and other professionals assisting in solving behavioral problems, understanding health problems, healing past traumas, and facilitating understanding between humans and animals. Kate has conducted classes, seminars and workshops throughout the United States and Europe.

Kate has contributed articles to *Animal Wellness, Tiger Tribe, Wolf Clan, Best Friends* and *Species Link* magazines. Kate is the author of several books on animal communication and holistic health. Her books have been translated into German, Italian, Czech, and Korean. Kate's work with animals has been featured in numerous books, journals and newspapers. Kate and her husband, Patrice Mattelon, are guest faculty members at The International School for Professional Horsemanship in Merle, Belgium teaching seminars on the human/horse relationship.

To learn more about Kate, or to schedule a personal consultation visit her website:

www.AKinshipwithAnimals.com

about
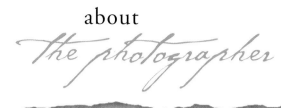
the photographer

TONY STROMBERG has worked as one of San Francisco's top commercial photographers for over a decade, photographing for clients such as The Gap, Banana Republic, Wells Fargo Bank, Gates Learjet, Boeing, Apple Computer, Intel, and Kodak.

Following an inner yearning for more space and stillness, Tony recently moved to Santa Fe to pursue his true passion in fine art photography and to be closer to his favorite subject, the horse. In working with the Bureau of Land Management, as well as numerous wildlife sanctuaries and private ranches, Tony travels throughout the western United States and Europe in search of the elusive and mysterious spirit of the wild horse, attempting to capture the freedom and power of his subjects on film.

His photography has been featured in several national publications, and is represented in numerous galleries throughout the United States. Tony also conducts equine-assisted personal growth and photography workshops in New Mexico. To learn more about Tony visit:

www.tonystromberg.com.

about

Council Oak Books

Since 1984 Council Oak Books has published books from all over the world, books that cross cultural lines to bring new understanding. Drawing from history, we publish for the future, presenting books that point the way to a richer life and a better world. Council Oak Books takes its name from a great oak tree, sacred to the Creek Indians, that still grows in the center of Tulsa, our home city. Our books are meant to inspire the sharing of knowledge in the quiet, contemplative space beneath the great Oak.

In keeping with this mission, we publish books on alternative health for animals, as well as the spiritual bond between humans and animals and other innovative titles on the relationship between humans and nature.

Please visit our website for a complete list of our current titles:

www.counciloakbooks.com